Stardust Dreams

Edited By Lynsey Evans

First published in Great Britain in 2024 by:

Young Writers
Remus House
Coltsfoot Drive
Peterborough
PE2 9BF
Telephone: 01733 890066
Website: www.youngwriters.co.uk

All Rights Reserved
Book Design by Ashley Janson
© Copyright Contributors 2024
Softback ISBN 978-1-83565-387-6

Printed and bound in the UK by BookPrintingUK
Website: www.bookprintinguk.com
YB0588S

FOREWORD

Welcome Reader, to a world of dreams.

For Young Writers' latest competition, we asked our writers to dig deep into their imagination and create a poem that paints a picture of what they dream of, whether it's a make-believe world full of wonder or their aspirations for the future.

The result is this collection of fantastic poetic verse that covers a whole host of different topics. Let your mind fly away with the fairies to explore the sweet joy of candy lands, join in with a game of fantasy football, or you may even catch a glimpse of a unicorn or another mythical creature. Beware though, because even dreamland has dark corners, so you may turn a page and walk into a nightmare!

Whereas the majority of our writers chose to stick to a free verse style, others gave themselves the challenge of other techniques such as acrostics and rhyming couplets.

Each piece in this collection shows the writers' dedication and imagination – we truly believe that seeing their work in print gives them a well-deserved boost of pride, and inspires them to keep writing, so we hope to see more of their work in the future!

CONTENTS

Abbots Farm Junior School, Rugby

Camilla Rourke (8)	1
Sai Eesha Manda (8)	2
Hermione Heyes (8)	3
Brencia James Pathinathan (8)	4
Rigveda Gohil (7)	5
Anastasia Hennessey (7)	6

Acomb First School, Acomb

Halle Bestford (7)	7
Gracie Robson (8)	8
Sophie Ward (9)	9
Ivy Lyall (9)	10
Anna Fabricius (8)	11
Rory Morshead (8)	12
Imogen Pardue (9)	13
Lucy Phillipson (9)	14
Skye Kirkby (9)	15
Daisy Hogg (7)	16
Charles Robson Stewart (8)	17
Noa Payne (8)	18
Adam Forsyth (9)	19
Daniel Wilson (8)	20
Emelia Thompson (8)	21
Isaac Johnson (7)	22
Alfie Strong (9)	23
Oscar Heaney (7)	24

Ashley Road Primary School, Aberdeen

Jiarun Yu (9)	25
Yvy Garza (8)	26

Ivy Onuoha (8)	28
Moez Soliman (8)	30
Morgane Emeriau (8)	31
Khang (Hans) Pham (8)	32
Bruno (8)	33
Adriana Kong (8)	34
Chiamaka Agbogu (8)	35
James Tulip (8)	36
Ali Belkouri (8)	37
Callum Lourie (8)	38
Jola Adebayo (7)	39
Marcus Amonoo (8)	40
Zoe Cruickshank (8)	41
Thomas Elliott (8)	42
Isabella Irvine (8)	43
Freddie Petrie (8)	44
Alanna Simpson (8)	45
Emma Cerda Carrascosa (8)	46

East Wittering Community Primary School, East Wittering

Grace Hills (10)	47
Elodie James (9)	48
Robyn Carney (10)	49

Gosberton Academy, Gosberton

Anthony Pearce Smith (8)	50
Ella Fouldes (8)	52
Holly Withers (8)	54
Eddie Scase (7)	55
Jasper Raven (9)	56
Eliza Ginger-Davis (8)	57
Lily Jessop (11)	58
George Barton (10)	59

Sana Dhilon Ahmed (10)	60
Isla Collins (10)	61
Macey Watson (9)	62
Leandra Rishan (7)	63
Roelan Rishan (9)	64
Holly Smith (9)	65
Reiss Ahmed (8)	66
William Edward Clark (11)	67
Evie-Rose Toon (9)	68
Ruby Verdegaal (9)	69
Jack Twelves (9)	70
Tyson Price	71
Scarlett Strathern (11)	72
Jessica Chatterton (8)	73
Austin George Clarke (10)	74
Freddie Sandall (8)	75
Reuben Sandall (10)	76
Hollie Gatward (8)	77
Francesca Lawrence (9)	78
Tobias Rudd (11)	79
Imogen-Marie Pratt (10)	80
Ella Palmer (11)	81
Joshua Twelves (11)	82
Lacey Fouldes (7)	83
Matthew Nunn (10)	84
Harry Collins (8)	85

Lodge Farm Primary School, Willenhall

Issabella Iris Campbell (11)	86
Abbie Price (11)	88
Beatrix Omorodion (10)	90
Arleta Narutyte (11)	91
Milosz Tur (10)	92
Ravjit Dhaliwal (7)	93
Taio Mason-Bernard (11)	94
Ivy-Marie Saxon (11)	95
Kierut Tank (10)	96
Harsukhman Singh (10)	97
Molly Hardy (8)	98

Macaulay Primary Academy, Grimsby

Bobby Short (9)	99
Sienna-rose Brown (9)	100
Amella Lee (9)	101
Tianna Corrigan (8)	102
Leila-Rose Stevenson (9)	103
Alexis Ann Johnson (8)	104
Silvie Turkova (8)	105
Khaleesi Skinner (9)	106

Nun Monkton Primary Foundation School, York

Rose Simpson (11)	107
Stanley Simpson (9)	108
George Shackleton (7)	109
Skyelah Stout (11)	110
Beatrice Tailby (9)	111
Florence Shackleton (9)	112
Winnie Jacob (10)	113
Jasper Burdette (10)	114
George Dunford (8)	115
Elijah Ritchie (9)	116
Ruby Buck (9)	117
Seb Burdette (10)	118
John Turton (7)	119

Orchard House School, Chiswick

Lottie Thorneycroft (9)	120
Iyla Stickney (9)	122
Lawrence Schmidt (10)	123
Michael Waller (10)	124
Amelia Arcos Lippens (9)	125
Thomas Jenke (10)	126
Theo Viall (9)	127
Theo Cleanis (10)	128
Antonio Maisto (10)	129
Harry Rees (10)	130
Louisa Fay (10)	131
Elsie Brimacombe (9)	132
Daniel Tovar (9)	133

Queen Eleanor Primary School, Harby

Scarlett Robson Rose (10)	134
Leila McCarthy (10)	135
Lawrence Bloor (10)	136
Freddie Baker (9)	137
George Barnard Hughes (10)	138
Ewan Jenkins (9)	139

Shepherd Primary School, Rickmansworth

Willow Finnegan (9)	140
Trishan Gupta (8)	142
Connie Moore (8)	144
Scarlett Jones (9)	146
Freddie Norwood (9)	147
Raeya Patel (8)	148
Leona Hetemi (8)	149
Thomas R (9)	150
Michael Swalwell (8)	151
Elis Byles (8)	152
Sariyah Thomas (9)	153

St Macartan's Primary School, Clogher

Niamh Hackett (11)	154
Aoibhe Meenan (11)	155
Aine McElroy (10)	156
Niamh Connolly (10)	157
Erin McKenna (10)	158
Ava McElroy (11)	159
Senan McElroy (10)	160
Alanagh Scott (11)	161
Darcy Keenan (9)	162
Eoin McConnell (9)	163
Enda Moynagh (10)	164
Fionnán Welford (10)	165

St Paulinus CE Primary School, Crayford

Harry Chester (6)	166
Thaniesh Seyon (6)	167
Lois Odelade (7)	168
Ara Ibukunolu (7)	169
Aubrey Gould (6)	170
Justin Fearon (7)	171
Niyah Lewis-Battiste (6)	172
Reggie King (6)	173
Theodore Tite (6)	174
Keziah Chege	175
Jacob Harding (7)	176
Darcy Lincoln (6)	177
Lily-Grace Garner	178
Roxie Fernandez	179
Zachariah Bolawole (6)	180
Imran Hussain (6)	181
Noelle Omotoso (7)	182
Ronnie King (6)	183
Jonatans Smirnovs (6)	184
Rumer Cotton (7)	185
Ethan Matthews (6)	186
Max Smith (7)	187
Billy Clarke (6)	188
Lily-Ann Wombell (7)	189

Steeton Primary School, Steeton

Farhan Hussain (11)	190
Mohammed Ehsan Jameel (11)	191
Mya Rodgers (10)	192
Emilia Quattrocchi (7)	193
Daisy Marley (11)	194

THE POEMS

Horse Adventure

Sunset brings a bright pink sky,
Time to saddle up and get ready to fly.
Lavender my horse is white and brown,
Her soft golden mane on her head is like a crown.

Elsie has a horse called Rose,
She is shiny black with a white patch around her nose.
Ivy has a horse called Poppy,
She is beautiful brown with ears that are floppy.

Off we gallop to the field of flowers,
It is so pretty I want to stay for hours.
We start to pick flowers the same name as the horse,
Lavender, Rose and Poppy of course.

I look at the sky, come on it's almost dark,
I hear a grasshopper sing; a dog bark.
I open my eyes I'm tucked up in bed,
My horse adventure was all in my head.

An exciting night trip, but it was only a dream,
I hope a horse of my own is what this can mean.

Camilla Rourke (8)
Abbots Farm Junior School, Rugby

Flying In The Starry Night

Excited, I gently lie in the freezing, quiet night,
Waiting patiently for the blinding, bright, magical light,
Now I am peacefully flying, watching the winking stars in the starry sky,
Peeking at the wise, blue bird gliding happily by,
Smiling cheekily, I lower myself down, down, down,
No ghastly nightmare, no greedy, spooky clown,
My flappy, pale nightgown now red as freshly picked roses,
I gracefully twirl around, then, like a dance, I add lots of fancy poses,
But slowly and sadly I start to disappear,
Maybe I will earn this amazing sensation next year...

Sai Eesha Manda (8)
Abbots Farm Junior School, Rugby

Dragon Life

Dragons live in the sky where we can't reach
It's very high and when they come back down below
They breathe their fire and make it glow
The dragon's cave is very cold
And it is filled with ores of gold
And this isn't any dragon
This is my dragon, Jimmy
And his favourite food is chilli
And he has purple spots
Or as you like to call them, dots
And he likes playing chess
And he loves buttons being pressed
And we travel around our world
With pumpkin cats and Pop-Tarts!

Hermione Heyes (8)
Abbots Farm Junior School, Rugby

Mickey Mouse

I'm in a forest I've never seen,
With a house which seems like a little bean.
I start shaking like a bat about to fly,
I see Mickey Mouse standing still about to cry.
He gives me a look straight in the eye,
And runs towards me like a dog,
That's seen a cat.
I fall and run as fast as can be...
And soon I wake up; it's all a dream.

Brencia James Pathinathan (8)
Abbots Farm Junior School, Rugby

The Magic Dancer

In a world of twirls and sparkle bright,
A magic dancer dances in the moonlight,
With ribbons swirling, a magic trance,
She twirls through the kingdom of magical chance,
Tiny toes tap on the stardust floor,
Spreading dreams, wanting more,
Her laughter echoes, a melody so sweet,
A magical dancer of wonder,
Dances in magic rhythm and beat.

Rigveda Gohil (7)
Abbots Farm Junior School, Rugby

Once Upon A Dream

This once upon a dream
Can this one dream about unicorns
Unicorns are beautiful and cute and amazing
Cute size and
Crazy too.

Unicorns, they are cute and good too
I am so cute
Unicorns too
Unicorns, amazing, good
So much good.

Anastasia Hennessey (7)
Abbots Farm Junior School, Rugby

A Pop Star's Dream

Last night when I went to bed
I had a thought upon my head
A thought, I said, but it was much more
As I walked through that open door.

I danced the night away
But to the people it was light of day
The plants started to grow
As they lit up my show.

I walked to the stage to sing a song
And the audience danced and sang along
Amazed to hear such beautiful sounds
These words I sang, this love I found.

I shone as bright as the stars in the sky
As I stood there smiling with a twinkle in my eye
Oh, how I did not want to wake from this dream
As it began to feel so real.

But as morning rose and I started to wake
I remembered how great it was to be on stage
So I will go to school and remember today
To dream tonight and sing away.

Halle Bestford (7)
Acomb First School, Acomb

My Pony Farm And Micro-Pig

In my world of hopes and dreams,
Where magic happens each day and night,
There is a farm where we all can play,
With the greenest of fields and the skies so blue,
Where hopes and dreams can always come true.

On this farm ponies are the best,
They canter and prance all puffing out their chests,
Oh, and on this farm is a micro-pig,
So tiny and cute with his snuffling snout and curly tail,
It makes my heart pound.

In this magical place where dreams come true,
I imagine myself from morning to night,
Riding the ponies each and every day,
And play with my pig,
It's the best of days.

So let's hold onto these dreams,
We hold so tight and work towards them with all our might,
And do hope one day these dreams come true.

Gracie Robson (8)
Acomb First School, Acomb

My Life As A Dream

I close my eyes and all is dark
I go to sleep with a dream
I dream for happiness
But it's not always how it seems.

I close my eyes and all is dark
But I go to a place where my dreams come true
In the woods is my place of peace.

I close my eyes and all is dark
In the woods I see brightness
I see creatures and animals messing around
And all the birds above swooping down.

I close my eyes and all is bright
In the morning I see sunlight
My family, my friends are all around!

I wake up and my dreams have come true
I wake up happy and I hope you do too!
Dreams do come true!

Sophie Ward (9)
Acomb First School, Acomb

Dreams In Our Hearts

They come at night
Once you turn off the light
Dreams will roam at midnight
Nightmares and dreams are very different
One is scary, and one isn't.

Puppies and cats may rain from the sky
Or you fly a kite with the sun shining bright
Or unicorns or rainbows
All dreams are amazing
Not silly or bad.

Anything can happen if you work hard
Wish upon a star it might come true
Wish for anything you want
So don't give up on anything
And if it doesn't come true
Don't worry eventually it will
Just have fun when you can
Even if your wishes don't come true.

Ivy Lyall (9)
Acomb First School, Acomb

If I Were A Dog For The Day

If I were a dog for the day,
I would go for a walk,
I might even chase a cat up a wall,
Then chase a ball.

If I were a dog for the day,
I would jump in the river with a splash!
When I'd get out I'd shake on my owner,
They would be as wet as a rock in a stream.

If I were a dog for the day,
I would sniff, sniff, sniff around,
And my owners would take me home to luxury.

If I were a dog for the day,
I would eat like a king on roast chicken,
And fall asleep whilst hogging the roaring fire.

Anna Fabricius (8)
Acomb First School, Acomb

My Sportsman Dream

I dream to be a sportsman,
I aim to be the best!
Sport is always in my brain.
Once my schoolwork is done, I go out to train.

Perhaps a footballer,
With three lions on my back.
Run and score and hit the top bin,
The crowd goes wild and the team is sure to win!

Perhaps a cricketer,
With my pads and hat.
Bat and bowl and take the wicket
And winning is the ticket.

Or a rugby star!
I will wear my shirt with pride.
Running like mad down the pitch, scoring the tries
And the other team cries.

Rory Morshead (8)
Acomb First School, Acomb

A Nightmare

In the dark, late at night,
I had a dream that gave me a fright.

All alone in a hazy fog,
I heard a growl and it wasn't a dog.

Twist and turny, it wasn't really right,
I put my hand forward and it felt like a bite.

Darkness fell upon me, I saw black and white,
A beast approached me so I hid out of sight.

Ring, ring, ring, my alarm clock rang,
I opened my eyes to see some fangs.

Looking down at me and licking my face... was my cute little pup,
Here to wake me up.

Imogen Pardue (9)
Acomb First School, Acomb

I Want To Be...

I want to be a black belt
I love to punch and kick
I like to practise every day
I am proud to wear my gi.

I want to work in a museum
History is my passion
I would love to curate
A World War I exhibition.

I want to be an explorer
To travel the whole wide world
I would meet lots of people and animals
And experience different cultures.

I want to always help people
And learn about their lives
I hope I am always a good friend
And I bring happiness to others.

Lucy Phillipson (9)
Acomb First School, Acomb

My Hopes And My Dreams

I hope one day I will get a dog,
To go walking in the fog,
I would get her bowl and put in the feed,
Then I would get her collar and clip on the lead.

My dream is to have a big house,
With some bunnies and maybe a mouse,
We would have some snuggles and have a cool play,
Then we would go out and enjoy our day.

When I grow up, I would like to be,
An author who writes with boundless energy,
Whilst I'm writing about my furry friends,
I hope the puppies won't chew all my pens.

Skye Kirkby (9)
Acomb First School, Acomb

I Have A Dream

I dream of fairies and unicorns,
Rainbow and sparkly lights,
I dream of playing with my friends,
On hot summer nights.

I dream of flowers and sunshine,
And looking for pots of gold,
I dream of princesses and fairy tales,
And *never* getting old.

I dream of floating,
On fluffy clouds in the sky,
I dream of being invisible,
And becoming a spy.

I dream of flying around the world,
And one day...
I dream of being a teacher,
And getting my own way!

Daisy Hogg (7)
Acomb First School, Acomb

Me And My Guitar

When I grow up I want to play the guitar,
I want to play music that makes people smile,
Maybe as part of a band or maybe on my own.
I don't really mind if I'm just playing it at home.

I hope to be as great as Angus Young,
He has inspired me through his amazing songs.

Who knows where me and my guitar will end up,
Hopefully playing my favourite song, 'Thunderstruck',
To hundreds of people,
And they'll be chanting, "Go, Charlie, go!"

Charles Robson Stewart (8)
Acomb First School, Acomb

Once Upon A Dream

Once I had a dream that I fell into a fairy tale,
I landed in a field full of candyfloss,
Trees, bushes and clouds,
With bubblegum-flavoured lollipop flowers.

The sun was made of vanilla ice cream,
And toffee sauce with a cherry on top.
I met a magical horse called Bella
And she had purple wings.

We flew over marshmallow mountains,
And saw a milkshake river,
With spinning fish made out of jelly.

Noa Payne (8)
Acomb First School, Acomb

My Dreams And My Goals

I want to be a millionaire
But not sat in my underwear
I want to be a YouTuber
But maybe when I've done that
I can fly to Vancouver.

I want a Lamborghini like the Joker
With a water gun on it as a soaker
I'll buy a season ticket to Newcastle United
I am very excited
But as long as I have my family
I know I'll be very happy.

Adam Forsyth (9)
Acomb First School, Acomb

Every Day There Is A New Adventure

One day I was walking down the street
And I came to the end of the road
What I did not know was it was the end of our world
Every day I came back until I walked past
And saw a big black hole
I kept walking until I told my friends
Eventually, another person saw it
We told the King
And ten years later I walked the other way.

Daniel Wilson (8)
Acomb First School, Acomb

Why Do We Have Dreams?

Sometimes I wonder why we have dreams
I normally dream of a place with lots of sunbeams
Sometimes I dream of being a dog
My mind then wakes up having a fog
But still, I don't have an answer
My mind is still doing a canter
But now I know that dreams are just imagination
They are just part of that beautiful creation.

Emelia Thompson (8)
Acomb First School, Acomb

My Hopes And Dreams

I dream of having a Ferrari F1, the colour is camo
And a big truck that roars.

I hope to be rich.

My dreamland has candy clouds and trees
The floor is candy, my house is Haribo
A sours river, lollipop flowers and chocolate mountains
The sun is ice cream
When it's cold the ice is ice lollies, yum.

Isaac Johnson (7)
Acomb First School, Acomb

Open A Book

Open a book and you will find a copper called Alfie,
One-of-a-kind,
Open a book and you can be a Bugatti driver,
Just like me,
Open a book and you can share dreams and aspirations all in the air,
Open a book and you will see my favourite pet,
A bearded dragon, cool and calm,
Just like me.

Alfie Strong (9)
Acomb First School, Acomb

Spooky Land

In Spooky Land the zombies are green as grass,
And their skeletons are made of brass,
They are in a forest with trees as tall as giants,
Their branches sticking out like arms waving at the zombies,
As they walk with a *stomp, stomp, stomp.*

Oscar Heaney (7)
Acomb First School, Acomb

Money Is Raining

I woke up to money,
It filled my whole house,
I forgot to tell you,
That Thomas E bought a mouse,
It was red and grey,
But the mouse in my dream was never found,
Ali and James were still sleeping,
Like a grizzly bear,
I called Thomas E to wake Ali up,
But the doorbell woke them up,
It was Hans at the door,
I was a cloud,
At least that's what I felt like,
But when I checked my bank account,
I found out I had infinite money,
I told them to change,
They asked, "Why?"
"I will explain on the way,"
I ordered a taxi, which was a limo,
To drive to the airport,
I told them that we were going to Vietnam,
But when I was flying over the sea,
I woke up in my bed!

Jiarun Yu (9)
Ashley Road Primary School, Aberdeen

Untitled

Something is weird,
I just can't put my mind to it,
All I see is lime and blue slime.
Lime is not the colour I like,
But I think it will be in need.

I take a step forward as nervous as can be,
My friend Kimberley is just what I might need,
Every step I take it feels insane,
Nervous like a hurricane,
Trying to eat me.

Darkness is not what I am looking for,
But the dancing clouds don't want to dance.
Running to Kim's house is not a bad idea,
"Wow," I gasp.

With each step I take I fall down,
Maybe I need some energy.
A dragon comes and attacks me,
This dragon is dangerous.

My friend Kim comes with lime slime,
Lime is not the colour I like,
But it might be in need.

Something strange happened,
I woke up to find myself in bed,
Safe at home.

Yvy Garza (8)
Ashley Road Primary School, Aberdeen

Magical Dream

Once upon a dream
I wake up on my bed
I realise that there is a mermaid-unicorn on my head
Thud
I land on a grass floor
I'm in the forest!
I see a fairy
As beautiful as a diamond
I can see magical unicorns
With twinkling bright horns
The trees dance in the wind
A gust of wind picks me up
As I close my eyes gently
I see a mouse nibbling on
My gingerbread house
I am in space
I feel a weird feeling
As I shoot out laser beams from my face
I see darkness take over
I fall to my knees
Bam! Bash!
He starts to use his powers to hit me!

I suddenly wake up
To realise this was just a magical dream
As I look at my puppy.

Ivy Onuoha (8)
Ashley Road Primary School, Aberdeen

The Battle

'Twas the time I woke up,
I looked up at the amazing beautiful sky that was as nice as a pizza,
Then, a morning chat with my friend James until a TV was nagging for long and long and long,
It said, "In time loop news, a bad guy has destroyed us in the future,"
I had to stop him,
A time loop ring portal,
I got James with me,
I saw him,
Bad guy in the futuristic battlefield,
He was an invincible man,
Bang!
I punched him with my fist,
"Kamehameha!" I shouted with fury,
He died and I was so angry,
Finally, just finally I beat him and everything was back to normal.

Moez Soliman (8)
Ashley Road Primary School, Aberdeen

My Dream Star

M y dream star is high in the sky
Y ou can think whatever you like

D reams and beliefs are as lovely as you and my star
R emember to be here close or far
E very day my star shines bright
A ll the time my star's as bright as the sun
M y heart goes *pump, pump, pump* around the star

S tar, my star, is so happy around me
T *ick-tock* goes the clock, I have less time
A ll dark and mesmerising the sky is tonight
R ight when I touch my bright beautiful star I wake up.

Morgane Emeriau (8)
Ashley Road Primary School, Aberdeen

Once Upon A Dream, I...

In my adventurous dream at night
I was in a gloomy, dark castle
When I walked on the floor, the floor creaked and the phone kept ringing
Then I saw a grumpy, gigantic ghost knight
It was chasing me all night and day
Then I got teleported to a different world
I was in the world of gods
Sitting in front of me was Zeus, sitting on a golden chair
The golden chair was as shiny as a light beam
Then a blue, old god grabbed me and it was about to stab me with its trident
But then I woke up and said, "Phew, it's just a dream."

Khang (Hans) Pham (8)
Ashley Road Primary School, Aberdeen

Trappist-1 System

T eleporting into a UFO,
R oaring loudly in it are,
A liens who are angry,
P ink bright lasers,
P inging like pingpong balls,
I t's the exhausts I see,
S itting in it are,
T eleportation machines, which walk and sit,
1 0 light-years now.

S ystem is as bright as the sun,
Y ou see, you see,
S ystem brighter,
T he UFO is a party room now,
"E veryone, go out," says the alien,
M ysterious, mystical, magic world.

Bruno (8)
Ashley Road Primary School, Aberdeen

Once Upon A Dream

Once upon a dream on a cloud, I see a big mansion,
Walls made of books, tests, pictures and jotters,
Beautiful and huge bedrooms.
A pretty big garden full of plants and wildlife,
Thousands of people live here and have lives,
Miss A, Mr Three, Mrs Drawing, Mr Book, Mr Test,
Mrs Flowers, who is a gardener.
I feel nervous like when I'm performing,
Strange gadgets and food.
Whoosh! A clown suddenly appears in front of me,
Making teachers laugh,
And a fairy comes and makes the clumsy, clever clown disappear...

Adriana Kong (8)
Ashley Road Primary School, Aberdeen

Mystical Unicorn

Once, on a magical day, a unicorn flew so high in the sky.
Beautiful wings, glimmering tail,
What a wonderful sight to see,
The shine of its horn reflecting on the floor made me wonder of stories untold,
Tail so bright, it flew so high,
I wondered how it felt up there in the sky.
I was so curious about what she could do,
Feeding her hay, letting her stay,
It was a dream come true, hum, hum!
Ice cream in my stomach.
Building my house with candy divine,
How I wished it could never end.

Chiamaka Agbogu (8)
Ashley Road Primary School, Aberdeen

Private Planes

Once upon a time,
I went on an amazing red
Private plane!
The plane was as big as the
Antanov 225!
When I get on the plane the
Chef was as fast as Sonic!
There was the
Burj Khalifa!
When I sat in my fabulous seat
I turned on the enormous, energetic, elegant TV,
With the black, fast remote control
Bang!
The TV was on!
The plane was an eagle in the sky,
I was on my way to the destination!

James Tulip (8)
Ashley Road Primary School, Aberdeen

Faris

A big, brave pirate called Sammy.
He's as brave as a shark.
He lives in a big city called Faris, the population is 40,000.
So he has to go on an adventure.
He goes climbing a mountain.
Suddenly, *boom!*
A chunk of the mountain falls.
I head to a cave.
He finds really divine emeralds.
Then he sees lots of creepy monsters.
He fights them and goes back to Faris and
Gets all the gems.

Ali Belkouri (8)
Ashley Road Primary School, Aberdeen

Peanuts

So, this is the world.
Okay, then, where are the flowers?
Where are the trees?
Where are the buzzing bees?

So, what's the point?
I just can't get my bearings.
Here, it's just a useless, boring bag of peanuts.
So, what's the point?

I'll just try again.
Oh, I just remembered.
My brother, Brian.
But, it's hopeless, he was my plan.

Callum Lourie (8)
Ashley Road Primary School, Aberdeen

Superpowers

In my dreams every night,
I have superpowers and might.
Like in some dreams,
Monsters come in shiny, shreddy beams.

They come and fight,
Throughout the night.
Zap! I shoot at them,
They all go as silent as REM.

Superpowers dancing around in the sky,
My dream was an explosion and the monsters died,
It was amazing, surprising, terrific and horrific!

Jola Adebayo (7)
Ashley Road Primary School, Aberdeen

Superman With No Friends

Superman is a hero
Defeating villains
And saving the world
No superhero friends
Maybe he will get a pet fish and pig
"I have a mansion
And ten bedrooms, two pools
And also twenty supercars
But no friends."
He gets a friend called the Flash
"Wait, a portal.
Who are you, a superhero?"

Marcus Amonoo (8)
Ashley Road Primary School, Aberdeen

Avery And The Cave

A little girl called Avery
It was damp, darkness, in a dark gloomy cave
She fell dangerously on the rock
The darkness floated above
She heard the darkness howl
It was catastrophic
It's a dark, windy darkness
Bang, crack, from above
It was like a pitch-black room
It was like a bomb site.

Zoe Cruickshank (8)
Ashley Road Primary School, Aberdeen

Aeroplane

A bsolute aeroplane crash site
E nd of nightmare is a long way away
R uins and wrecks all around me
O h no!
P lanes going *crash!*
L ong way from home
A nd missing my friends
N ightmares are bad
E nd of nightmare, *yay!*

Thomas Elliott (8)
Ashley Road Primary School, Aberdeen

Monsters

M y mind is filled with mischievous, massive monsters.
O h! My dream is angry with me!
N ow, thrash the spider army. Is a band playing?
S aved by monster!
T ime to go!
E very day, I think about the
R ed and blue monster.
S o I go back next year.

Isabella Irvine (8)
Ashley Road Primary School, Aberdeen

Tennis

Every night in my dreams I dream of being a super amazing tennis player.
I dream of being the best one yet!
In the dream, I was at the Wimbledon final.
Playing amazing Alcaraz I felt as happy as could be.
Wimbledon's grass was as soggy as soil.
Alcaraz took the first shot, it was as hard as ice.

Freddie Petrie (8)
Ashley Road Primary School, Aberdeen

My Nightmare

I can see a small pretty unicorn,
Her hair is like a colourful rainbow,
I am in a gingerbread house with sweets on top,
I walk out the door, suddenly I hear bangs,
I run to my house and run upstairs,
I look out the window and see everyone is there!

Alanna Simpson (8)
Ashley Road Primary School, Aberdeen

I Have Dreamed: Monster High

I'm with my cousins
And unexpectedly there's a door
With a human hand
After, I put my hand on the door
And the door opens
With my cousin, I go downstairs
Downstairs are fossils
And after, I go upstairs to see his mum.

Emma Cerda Carrascosa (8)
Ashley Road Primary School, Aberdeen

My World

In my world, where my dreams live, all my sad thoughts fly away.
As soon as I play my favourite song,
All the butterflies glide along.
Everybody knows my name,
I really enjoy all this fame.
But before I knew it, it would all end,
But in my world the fun never descends!
Everywhere I looked I could see my friends
They all smiled and said, "You're the best."
Mia and Paige were eating their lunch,
I said, "Can I join?"
And they said, "Of course, there's always enough."
In my world where my idols live
They always say, "You can do anything!"
I sometimes believe them, I sometimes don't
But I always remember that I should definitely try.
In my world where my dreams live
I now wake up and a new day begins.

Grace Hills (10)
East Wittering Community Primary School, East Wittering

Nofalofagus

Lost in the galaxy
Only planets and stars
Alien Bean Bodies
Looking for home
Nofalofagus!

Alien Bean Bodies, Boops and Zoo-Zoo
Tom, Linti and Derrick
All smell of sweets.
Linti smells minty.
Boops smells like toffee.
Tom's pink and white and smells like candy cane.

Zoo-Zoo smells of green gummy bears
And rides a shooting star.
She's a skunky monkey.
Derrick is the bossy leader
And Linti's just sassy
And they're all looking for home
Nofalofagus!

Elodie James (9)
East Wittering Community Primary School, East Wittering

Dreaming

When I go to sleep at night,
I see a great light.
With dragons roaring,
And artists drawing.
Pirates saying, "En garde,"
Whilst children are getting lost in a yard.

People with superpowers,
Whilst pulling up their trousers.
Monsters destroying,
And clowns yawning.

Royalty having coronations,
Whilst builders create door relations,
Anything is what it can seem,
When you are in a dream!

Robyn Carney (10)
East Wittering Community Primary School, East Wittering

Racing Cars

I close my eyes, after a while darkness fades
All of a sudden, I am near the arcade
I see cars doing amazing things
Oh the excited feelings it brings
Zooming past at supersonic speed
Doing tricks, stunts and things you won't believe
So many colours appear as blurry streaks
All the time the highest score trying to beat
Black, yellow, orange, red, white, silver, green and blue,
Drivers collecting and drinking bright colour goo
It looks like toxic waste
Who knows how it might taste
Each drink gives you different superpowers
Is it made from herbs and special flowers?
You can be a villain or hero
Make a crew of family, friends or foes
Commit the ultimate betrayal
Or be the hero who won't fail
It's my turn to pick my car and race
A black and white supercar is my base
Flaming stickers and lightning bolt details
With fire coming from the rear exhaust tail
Neon lights dancing underneath

Keeping in time with the music beat
Zooming ever faster round the multicoloured track
Collecting powerups and weapons to throw back
Trying to stay way out in the lead
YouTubers commenting on the news feed
My custom supercar is getting a lot of attention
It's me who's driving but I don't get a mention
The race is soon over with me coming first
I'm so happy I could literally burst
In my dream, my skills were put to the test
I proved to everyone, I am the best
As all around me clap and cheer
For having a score no one can come near
The sound and colours start to merge and disappear
A far distant calling, I begin to hear
Louder and louder, clearer and clearer
Reality is calling and getting nearer
Next thing I know, I am in my bed
Rubbing my eyes and shaking my head
It's time to wake up and get ready for school
I smile all through the morning as my dream was so cool.

Anthony Pearce Smith (8)
Gosberton Academy, Gosberton

Nan's House!

One day, I was lying in my bed
And wonderful things filled my head like...
Today, I went to my nan's house,
And she was trying to chase a mouse.

Once we caught it, Nan put it outside,
But she told me to wait outside.
First, I wandered around for a while
And then I spotted a broken tile.

I went to go and lift it up
But then I ended up with a cut.
As soon as it happened, I put the tile down,
And then in the cupboard, I spotted a clown.

Instead of a clown, it was a clown book,
But when I pulled half out, it had a scary look.
I tried to pull it out but it was stuck,
Although, in the future, I had some luck.

Suddenly, the entire bookshelf moved three spaces forward.
It left a little space for me to peek around, but it was tiny and awkward.

Then, I found another book and it was Tom Gates,
Then it all came straight forward like a little race.

Once I got in, I smiled with a grin.
There was a potion above my head,
But when I woke up I was in bed.

Ella Fouldes (8)
Gosberton Academy, Gosberton

The Night Of Evil

'C ause I had gone to bed, I started dreaming
L ater in my dream, scary things happened
O n me was a hat, a red hat
W here was I? I didn't know
N ow I was scared and alone
S oon I heard a noise.

W here was that noise coming from?
E ventually, it stopped, but little did I know bad things were coming
R ooms were around me
E ven though I was scared, I was alone too.

C ould I escape?
H ad I left my dream?
A noise came, and so did clowns and monsters
S oon, they were chasing me
I n a flash, they caught up
N ow my heart was pounding, but then they disappeared
"G o," said a voice.

M y body stopped, and before I could look down, I was gone
E ven though it was a dream, I was terrified.

Holly Withers (8)
Gosberton Academy, Gosberton

Down In The Forest

Dawn in the forest we are off to build a den,
Although I like exploring I realise we are lost again,
All of a sudden I start to yell,
I spot a unicorn who might help,
She asks me to hop on up, it is really scary,
She's taking me to see the Sparkles, the fairy,
We gallop past trees, toadstools and gnomes,
Off in the distance, I can see tiny fairy houses,
Sparkles comes to greet us in a gorgeous pink dress,
Everybody is so nice and really impressed,
We eat and talk, I am feeling a lot less scared,
It is really nice that so many people care,
Today has been a really long one, and I have a sleepy head,
The fairies work as a team to build me a nice comfy bed,
I close my eyes and start to snore,
Suddenly, I hear a knock on my door,
I open my eyes and it would seem,
That my fairy bed was just a dream.

Eddie Scase (7)
Gosberton Academy, Gosberton

The Village Of St Harold

Here in my village, there are people everywhere.
Some people over here and some people over there.
There are cooks who make delicious food,
The cobblers make comfy shoes.

Musicians playing a lovely harp,
Blacksmiths making the axes sharp.
The armour helmets are strong, to say the least!
The warriors fight before they feast,

The farmers out there, shearing their sheep.
Weavers making soft bed sheets.
Happy children playing around.

Girls helping around the house.
Boys learning their fathers' skills,
Like attacking enemies and hunting on hills.

Our leader and king sitting on his throne.
I love my village! I'll never leave home!

Jasper Raven (9)
Gosberton Academy, Gosberton

Dream Big Dreams

Dream big dreams every night,
I know it's dark, so don't get the frights!
Dream about unicorns and dream about fairies
Dream about lions and dream about Mayans!
Go to bed, it's time to sleep,
Shut your eyes and start to swim deep!
You know your parents are just downstairs,
So you don't have to be afraid of bears!
Dream big dreams every night,
Don't get scared because you've got a light!
Touch the stars in the sky,
Then watch fairies start to fly!
Dreams are fairies just floating in the sky,
Getting ready to disappear,
And make sure you're *happy* and full of *joy!*

Eliza Ginger-Davis (8)
Gosberton Academy, Gosberton

Dream Or Nightmare

As I lie in bed
I think, where shall I go tonight?
Will I go to monsters that bite?
Or even play with fairies that fly
High above the sky?
Where will I go?
No one will know.

As my mind finally drifts
I begin to fly up and up
As I look down I see everything shrink and finally disappear
I lie on a cloud with creatures surrounding me.

The sky begins to deepen as if horror music plays
And I feel petrified, unsure of what will happen.

I hear a door open
But there are no doors up there.
But it's just my mum checking I'm okay.
At least I know that she will care.

Lily Jessop (11)
Gosberton Academy, Gosberton

TV Of Terror

I turned on the TV and watched the news
Then the TV went blank and made me very confused
The next thing I knew I was sat next to Peter Levy
And he was reading out the news
He was very startled when he saw me.

But I realised I still had the remote
So I changed the channel to Virgin Radio
And they were talking about a flea.

Again the TV went white and
I was sat next to Graham Norton
He thought it was a prank
I changed the channel and
It was a show about making planks.

You know what?
I've had enough of this TV of terror
I'm going back to bed.

George Barton (10)
Gosberton Academy, Gosberton

I Want To Be A Famous Football Player!

I want to be a famous football player!
If I was, I would make my family proud.
I would have superpowers so I could hear people who bet on me.
I could make bets come true!
People who try and tackle me,
They stand no chance against me.
Sometimes, people who don't know how to play, I'll go easy on them.
But people who know how to play, I will not go easy on them!

The reason I like and want to be a famous footballer
Is because it is entertaining.
I want to be like Ronaldo, Neymar Junior and Mbappé!
So I hope I become extremely famous
Just like Ronaldo, my role model!

Sana Dhilon Ahmed (10)
Gosberton Academy, Gosberton

My Nightmare Teacher

In my nightmares as well as at school
They stand above me very tall
Crooked noses and greasy hair
Mean and evil wicked glares
Simultaneously they all shout at me
"Where's your homework? Do it quickly!"
The head one comes above us all
Throwing out homework like it's a netball
It's like they're aliens that come from Mars
And want to put us behind jail bars
I hope and hope they won't haunt me
But they just won't leave me be

So when I go to school tomorrow
Will I find my teacher is a creature within?

Isla Collins (10)
Gosberton Academy, Gosberton

Pokémon World

P is for Pikachu,
O is for Oshawott,
K is for Keldeo,
E is for Electrode,
M is for Mimi Lugia,
O is for Oddish,
N is for Necrozma.

W is for Wartortle,
O is for Onix,
R is for Raichu,
L is for Leavanny,
D is for Darkrai.

Charmander is red,
Squirtle is blue,
If you were a Pokémon,
I'd choose you.

Yveltal is red,
Xerneas is blue,
Fennekin is cute,
But not as cute as you!

Macey Watson (9)
Gosberton Academy, Gosberton

Sleeping On The Beam

Sometimes I have the best dream
Every gym day on the beam,
But then one night my dream came true,
I was in a gymnastics stadium - everything was blue.

There stood Kyla Ross,
As she stood there she looked like the boss,
As she saw me she came down to say hi,
I came to her and I said bye.

The next minute I was called on the speaker,
Even while I was wearing sneakers,
While I was doing a simple routine,
The judges thought I was the queen.

In the end, I won two gold medals and three silver medals.

Leandra Rishan (7)
Gosberton Academy, Gosberton

My Fortnite Dream

I boot up my PC,
Then log in to Fortnite.
My duo invites me.
Then all of a sudden,
I get sucked into Fortnite.

We meet on Spawn Island,
Deciding where to drop.
We tell each other where we'll land
On the Fortnite map.

We land at Lavish Lair
And collect some shields.
But then we see a pair,
So we strike.

We defeat Oscar, get the medallion,
And notice there are four players left.
They create a huge attraction,
And then we get the win.

Roelan Rishan (9)
Gosberton Academy, Gosberton

If Dogs Could Fly

If dogs could fly, where would they go...?
To Italy, to see the Leaning Tower of Pisa?
To Spain, to eat the amazing paella?
They'd fly over mountains and through candyfloss clouds.
Off to Colombia where the coffee beans grow...
To have a cuppa with the Queen,
Then home again to have more doggy dreams!

People say that they have not seen this amazing, bizarre, flying thing.
A waggy tail and fluffy rainbow wings.
Have you seen a flying dog in your dreams?

Holly Smith (9)
Gosberton Academy, Gosberton

In A Magical World

In a magical world
Where mysterious creatures
And mythical people lurk around
Dragons, monsters and even royal wizards
Come together to fight a powerful, evil witch
Dragons flying up and down
Wizards running left to right
Monsters jumping on bouncy clouds
Having fun all around
The witch is horrified to see this display
Then I wake up in my room
Realising it was only a magical dream
Now it's time to get ready for school.

Reiss Ahmed (8)
Gosberton Academy, Gosberton

Hockey Player

      C **H** arging onto the field.
Nerv **O** usly taking my position.
      C hancing my career with a shot.
      K nowing I've made the right decision.
      E xcitedly celebrating.
      Y earning to be the best.

      P laying with my friends.
      L earning as I go from club to club.
      A chieving great awards.
      Y elling crowds, erupting stadium.
   R **E** aching the end of a match.
Victo **R** y!

William Edward Clark (11)
Gosberton Academy, Gosberton

Nightmares

N ightmares are terrible
I n the night you have a nightmare or dream
G host floating around
H aunted house next to you
T errible witches flying in the sky
M onsters under your bed
A nd terrible thoughts in your head
R unning as fast as can be
E ast, west, north, south but nobody was out
S piders running up your legs but you wake up safe, in your bed.

Evie-Rose Toon (9)
Gosberton Academy, Gosberton

All About Me!

My favourite animal is a koala.
My favourite food is a doughnut.
My favourite movie is Harry Potter.
And I love to do gymnastics!

I love to jump up and down,
I love to turn around!
I love to be happy
But sometimes I can be a bit sassy!

My favourite drink is pink lemonade.
I love to play games.
I love to play with my pets
And make them have the best day!

All about me!

Ruby Verdegaal (9)
Gosberton Academy, Gosberton

Space Ball

Once upon a time, there was a boy called Nate,
Who lived with his mate,
But it's not where you think it is,
It's up in space,
The boy wanted a job,
He wrote and wrote,
And suddenly got a reply,
They said Nate was the guy,
On the message, it said 'do you want to join the space league?'
Nate said it was a dream,
But it wasn't and he got his favourite job.

Jack Twelves (9)
Gosberton Academy, Gosberton

Untitled

As cool as Ronaldo
As sweet as his goals
How does he do it?
No one recalls
He shoots like an animal
And sees like a bell
Everyone is tackling
But intel
He shoots
He scores
And then he roars
He shoots off the floor
That makes everyone shout, "Score!"
We need to know when he will strike again
But then we wait when
He rises again.

Tyson Price
Gosberton Academy, Gosberton

The Monster Under The Bed

Under the bed, there is a weird-looking thing;
Big round eyes, long spiked legs, with a long speared tail.
It pokes out from under the bed
It switches from bed to bed
There is a *monster* under the bed!
Who crawls out at exactly 3am every morning.

Nobody dares to stay awake,
Nobody dares to look under the bed,
Because nobody knows what's next!

Scarlett Strathern (11)
Gosberton Academy, Gosberton

What Does Dad Dream About?

I always wonder what my dad dreams
Could he be dreaming about winning the lottery or flying to space?
Could his dreams be filled with giant cream cakes or winning the World Cup?
Could he be dreaming of a giant roast dinner or a yummy fried breakfast?
Could he be dreaming of me and my bro, or days in the future as we grow and grow?
Whatever he dreams, I do hope they come true.

Jessica Chatterton (8)
Gosberton Academy, Gosberton

Goal!

I stand on the field with my heart beating fast,
Anxiously waiting for my teammate to pass.
So I make my run into space,
I beat the best defender with my outstanding pace.

I take my first look, should I shoot or should I pass?
There's only a keeper to beat!
So let's make this fast!
All the parents roaring! I shoot and...
Goal!

Austin George Clarke (10)
Gosberton Academy, Gosberton

Football!

F ootball playing as a team
O ffside is a rule we don't play
O f course, the goalie saves the day
T ackling and defending is how we play
B elting the ball in the back of the net
A ll my friends, we make a solid team
L ose or win, we are just happy we played
L unchtime matches are my favourite!

Freddie Sandall (8)
Gosberton Academy, Gosberton

Football With Friends

Football is my favourite sport,
Gosberton Academy, top of the leaderboard.
Me and my friends play this game,
In all sorts of weather - wind, sun and rain.
Putting on our kits and playing as a team,
Winning the league is our dream.
Mr Baxter training us and shouting from the side,
He cried as the ball went wide.

Reuben Sandall (10)
Gosberton Academy, Gosberton

Friends

I have a magic fairy,
Her name is Tinker Bell,
She rides a special unicorn,
He is my friend as well,
We go on magical adventures as often as we can,
We go to visit our friend whose name is Peter Pan,
We travel through the clouds and in the forest too,
You never know, we may come to visit you.

Hollie Gatward (8)
Gosberton Academy, Gosberton

Me And My Team

Me and my team getting ready to go out,
Me and my team ready to shout!
Me and my team set the level high,
Me and my team smash it to the sky!
Me and my team hit zero,
Me and my team were the new heroes!
To the awards here we come,
We got first place, my team and I got the job done!

Francesca Lawrence (9)
Gosberton Academy, Gosberton

Once Upon A Dream

I want to be part of a team,
To handle the ball with control,
To score the winning goal,
I'll be running down the wing,
I'll be treated like a king,
I'll play with Bellingham,
I'll free-kick like Beckham,
This is my dream,
Once upon a dream.

Tobias Rudd (11)
Gosberton Academy, Gosberton

Aromas From The Bakery

Doughnuts, cinnamon rolls, white icing,
Aromas from the bakery wafting.
My dream of owning my own place to bake,
Sometimes, I don't want to wake.

Taking hold of my imagination,
Wanting to showcase my creation.
My desire to bake,
Really scrummy cake.

Imogen-Marie Pratt (10)
Gosberton Academy, Gosberton

Living In A Dream

In my dream, I'm stuck between book pages,
Swimming through blue sparkling seas,
Galloping through trees,
I have a pet called Hallie,
Who keeps a tally of all our adventures,
My heart skips a beat every night we meet,
But then I realise it's just a dream.

Ella Palmer (11)
Gosberton Academy, Gosberton

Daydream Devil

Once upon a time
There was a daydream devil
A daydream devil who had a tail
He had horns bright red
And tail dark red
But *don't* get the wrong side of him
He's as fast as a cheetah and as eager as an owl
And suddenly... I got caught.

Joshua Twelves (11)
Gosberton Academy, Gosberton

Dinosaur

I can see my dinosaur
My big green dinosaur
Playing in the forest
We are a little bit lost
Walking through the forest
With crunchy leaves
And tall trees
Squishy mud and blowing wind
We find our way home.

Lacey Fouldes (7)
Gosberton Academy, Gosberton

Rainy Night

Raindrops, raindrops,
It's a rainy night,
It's rained cats and dogs,
It's rained, poured and drizzled,
And chucked it down,
Rain, rain go away,
And bring me a rainbow.

Matthew Nunn (10)
Gosberton Academy, Gosberton

Tedd

This is my monster and his name is Tedd.
He comes out at night from under my bed.
He messes up my room and jumps on my bed!
This is my monster and his name is Tedd.

Harry Collins (8)
Gosberton Academy, Gosberton

A Lost Dream

Once a lost dream,
I saw clouds and stars,
I was in a forest,
Entering alone - or was I?

I followed a path of stardust,
The further I went,
The more lost I seemed.

I thought I was being watched,
So I turned around,
Seeing a girl,
Her name was 'Rin', she said.

She held a fennec fox pocket,
It looked like a locket,
I paused seeing the lady.

She was beautiful,
She held an instrument, a biwa,
I stared, amazed.

She was silent and still,
Like a statue,

We walked past silently,
I saw a light.

Was this the end?
As we approached the light,
It became bright.

We parted,
Just as I departed,
I woke up,
I felt like a lump.

Maybe she will return,
Maybe she won't,
A very silent night,
Falling back into a dream world...

Issabella Iris Campbell (11)
Lodge Farm Primary School, Willenhall

A Dream Of A Field

I sit in a field where brooks and rivers flow
And the rivers aren't raging
At all, they are very very slow,
I begin to feel curious
And awareness begins to dim
I stand up and go for a little stroll.
I can hear the birds and bees
As they buzz through the trees.
I look round the corner
And what do I see?
Big and small dragons asleep;
I wander closer to get a closer peek.
But oh no!
There is one dragon awake now
I feel like my life is at stake...
Have I made a big mistake?
But no, when the dragon comes towards me,
My fear begins to shrink
It lets me ride on its back but then I start to think,
Is this all a dream?
I jolt up

I'm still in my bed
I lie back down and turn my head
Can I carry on my dream instead?

Abbie Price (11)
Lodge Farm Primary School, Willenhall

Magical Dreams

In a land full of magic where things aren't tragic,
I wander freely, where anything can be,
My heart filled with pride, taking the bad things aside,
I believe in myself, and the dreams I behold.

Up the hills, white, fluffy snowflakes drop,
Snow falling down nonstop,
Rustling noises, my boots crunching the snow on the ground,
It's a nice place but I still want to be found.

Evergreen trees, bright falling leaves,
I slightly roll down my sleeves,
A colourful journey, forever shining bright,
From the reality of wonder, the dream plays with light.

In hues of crimson and gold, my dreams unfold,
Stars bright as a diamond across the baby blue sky,
It's time I don't deny,
But it's time I should say goodbye.

Beatrix Omorodion (10)
Lodge Farm Primary School, Willenhall

The Meadow

I sit in a tranquil meadow
As calm and peaceful as it can possibly be,
A scared land free of sin,
And flowers stretching as far as the eye can see.

I make a flower crown of many different flowers,
And place it on the head of the semi-transparent spirit,
My hair covers my face as I softly laugh,
Admiring this place I constantly revisit.

We gently step over to the crystal-clear steam,
It glistens in the sun, a blinding gleam,
I cup my hands and dip them into the water,
Sipping the liquid which is reassuringly clean.

Sadly, it is now my time to leave,
I wave my friend goodbye, the wreath still around her head,
A hurricane of butterflies now surrounds me,
And just like that, I am back in my bed.

Arleta Narutyte (11)
Lodge Farm Primary School, Willenhall

Once A Lucid Dream...

A very, very long time ago,
There was once a kid named Moe,
He once had a dream where he was in a graveyard,
And in his pocket, he had a card,
Escape for mercy.

He ran for his life,
He looked down and saw a knife,
He was still scared for his life,
Moe started to explore with the knife.

Moe started to hear screaming,
Until... he saw someone peeping,
He started running and never looked back,
Every tombstone had a crack.

The monster started to catch up,
Moe started to slow down,
He slipped on a rock,
The monster was behind him.

The monster got Moe,
He suddenly woke up in his bedroom,
Alone.

Milosz Tur (10)
Lodge Farm Primary School, Willenhall

Midnight Dream

D eep down in a jungle
R eally lots of people need to die
E verywhere lots of dinosaurs fly
A lways people die
M onsters in the night, they give you
S uch a fright!

I n the dreams they give you such a sprite
N obody can escape, except from dying

T he island monsters are chasing me
H earts are beating to escape
E nd of the hell never happens

N ight time is their playtime
I n the night it gives me such a fright
G oing to escape is a nightmare!
H ello the devil is going to say
T his is the never-ending maze of hell, this is a world of fright.

Ravjit Dhaliwal (7)
Lodge Farm Primary School, Willenhall

Mythical Worlds

Once upon a time there was a girl
A girl named Emilie, she was a lovely
Dreamful girl who loved imagination

She once walked into a portal
Emilie found lots of her friends
Then dragons flew in the night
Nice and bright in the sky

Beautiful rainbows changing multiverse
As they sway through the earth
Plants grow whilst dragons flow
Seeing the night stars as they go
Dragons growing, Earth is flowing
Dogs ruffing while birds are calling
Children playing whilst they sway around Earth.

Taio Mason-Bernard (11)
Lodge Farm Primary School, Willenhall

Cemetery!

I live in a cemetery,
That is full of people's memories,
Ghosts are near,
I think I can hear,

I live in a cemetery,
The wind is flowing,
I hear thunder,
There is no lightning,
But there is crying,

I live in a cemetery,
Where I can still hear crying.
But I might have a sleep in,
Or maybe I should go near,

I live in a cemetery,
There is no more crying,
Just some barking,
Back down in the grave.

Ivy-Marie Saxon (11)
Lodge Farm Primary School, Willenhall

Reality

Across the dark multiverse,
With a collapsing reality,
Me and my special crew,
As we search and go through.

All around peculiar scenes,
Ripples gather all around,
We shall hurry down,
Or we will go down.

Cracks in the sky,
Where is the sky?
Time frozen in midair,
One path to reality.

Two black holes following the crew,
I wish I flew,
I am there now through,
But why are there animations everywhere?

Kierut Tank (10)
Lodge Farm Primary School, Willenhall

Space Journey

S o, I wake up in a spaceship,
P eculiar creatures surround me,
A misty breeze in the air,
C overing all of my surroundings,
E verlasting confusion.

J elly coloured fantasy,
O ur journey has not ended yet,
U ntil our space dog is rescued.
R eality starts to creep in,
N o one to be seen,
E nding our dream,
Y ellow space puppy cannot be seen.

Harsukhman Singh (10)
Lodge Farm Primary School, Willenhall

Once Upon A Nightmare

N ight time is very dark
I t all lights up when you light a spark
G ood and bad come out
H owever they don't make a noise, not even a pout
T he dragons fly in the midnight sky
M y dreams are great, just like pie
A re dreams bad? No one knows
R eally dark sky
E very night my imagination comes to life
S uper fun crazy dreams.

Molly Hardy (8)
Lodge Farm Primary School, Willenhall

My Journey Through Space

I laid down my head and went to sleep,
I fell down a hole that was very, very deep.
It was as deep as the ocean, as dark as the sky,
I fell and fell but I began to fly.
I flew all the way to space,
But my heart started beating; it began to race.
I saw the stars and the planets with the space centre too!
A UFO flew past, the alien was blue,
It had one big, black eye and a hole for its nose,
It had razor-sharp teeth and was missing its clothes.
I sat on a star, right next to the moon,
I looked down in fright as the path went boom!
Blood was running to my head,
It was such a relief to wake up in my bed.

Bobby Short (9)
Macaulay Primary Academy, Grimsby

The Swing

One sunny morning,
I saw the wind fly by,
And it pushed me a little,
But then someone helped it.

I felt very uncomfortable,
They were pushing me really hard,
So I fell off the chain,
That was holding me up.

And when I fell to the ground,
I started to cry.
The wind picked up my sound,
And dropped it into the sea.

And then the wind came back to me,
And dropped me into the sea,
And that was the end of me.

Sienna-rose Brown (9)
Macaulay Primary Academy, Grimsby

Untitled

One day a girl was told not to go into the forest
Because a boy had got lost
So she went to bed but couldn't sleep
She got up and went to the forest

It was dark at night and windy
So got a bit scared
All of a sudden she heard the boy scream
She started to run and cry

She heard two boys
One screaming, one shouting
She saw a boy with a cut
She got out fast and went back to bed safely.

Amella Lee (9)
Macaulay Primary Academy, Grimsby

The Shooting Star

Once I saw a shooting star out of the window, but let it go.
I felt the fluffy clouds from the moonlit sky.
I heard the same vibrating sound.
I got lonely as it was just the shooting star and me.
I watched the sunset come down.
The only thing that was left after the sunset was the lonely shooting star itself.

Tianna Corrigan (8)
Macaulay Primary Academy, Grimsby

Untitled

Once there was a cat that went *purr, purr, purr*.
Once there was a bear that had fur, fur, fur.
Once in the forest,
They stumbled upon an orthodontist.
He checked their jaws,
Their teeth were okay for sure.
They said, "Bye and thank you,"
For making sure they were alright.

Leila-Rose Stevenson (9)
Macaulay Primary Academy, Grimsby

The Spider

I am a spider that nobody cares about,
I am a happy old spider with no friends,
So it's going to come to my end soon,
I would normally fly away with Peter Pan,
And the trees dance as I sit down,
In the trees as I watch Peter Pan fly away with Tinker Bell.

Alexis Ann Johnson (8)
Macaulay Primary Academy, Grimsby

The Land Of Dragons

One night, a boy had a dream about going on a hike.
"Argh!" He saw a dragon pointing his sharp teeth toward him.
He began to run then he finally woke up
And he looked under his bed and saw dinosaurs
And ran out of bed like it was not even rare.

Silvie Turkova (8)
Macaulay Primary Academy, Grimsby

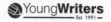

The Wind

I'm the wind
No one can see me flying past
Sometimes nice and gentle
When I am angry, I blow a gale
Nice and strong where I can blow a tree down
Seeing waves crash and things flying
When I am in a stormy mood.

Khaleesi Skinner (9)
Macaulay Primary Academy, Grimsby

The Man With Blue Eyes

He hustles around a moonlit table,
I peer around as much as I am able,
On his desk, a collection of jars rattle and shake,
Their spinning colours looking like the sea in a quake,
Inside are bubbling hues, rainbows of blue,
Oranges, reds, pinks and yellows too,
On his desk are carefully sketched designs,
Of my throbbing, pink, wrinkled mind,
Then I realise the strangest thing of all,
These are all my dreams – things I recall,
The jars glisten in the moonlight, letting out muffled calls,
As the maker turns around,
He lets out a gravelly screeching sound,
His eyes light up an electric blue,
As he says, "Beware, you,"
With an alarming click of his finger,
I am sent to my dreams, no time to linger,
And now as the night draws in,
I think of that man and – what happened to him?

Rose Simpson (11)
Nun Monkton Primary Foundation School, York

Will I Ever Get Out Of Here?

I stumbled and fell as the light started to flicker,
I felt my heart, it beat quicker and quicker.
My brain in my head throbbed and bubbled
As my mind doubled and doubled.
I thought and thought, *will I ever survive*
Or maybe even revive?
An arrow whizzed past and hit a tree,
And it revealed a key.
I grabbed it and jabbed it into a stone,
Which opened a portal to a cone,
And made itself turn into a chair,
Which hovered in mid-air.
Then I thought, *it's a dream*,
But then he did a scream,
Which hit my ear,
And made me tremble with fear.
Will I ever get out of here?

Stanley Simpson (9)
Nun Monkton Primary Foundation School, York

Wizard

W ill it fly or will it sigh? The dark purple magic cloak will make the fizzing, whizzing potions
I watch in fear but never as the wizard's black furry cat stares in anger
Z ooming blooms always win, the long-bearded wizard looks down from the dark gloomy sky
A stunning potion is an amazing success on the day it's tested, it turns people to stone
R oaming villagers, children playing I-Spy, looking at the sky in astonishment while it flies by
D aring potions finish the dusty drawer, right behind the door creaking, the wizard's here.

George Shackleton (7)
Nun Monkton Primary Foundation School, York

Woodland Of Wonder

I walked towards a woodland of wonder
Where not a single cloud had any thunder
And beaming ruby-red mushrooms
Where no one assumes
Who you should or shouldn't be
I felt all of a sudden so free
Once upon a dream.

I walked towards a woodland of wonder
Where vines swirled around trees
And every flower had many bees
I skipped and stumbled through the sun-dappled leaves
Where all you had to do was truly believe
My insides were jumping up and down enthusiastically
And my aqua-blue wings shot up fantastically
Once upon a dream.

Skyelah Stout (11)
Nun Monkton Primary Foundation School, York

I Dreamt I Was In Finland

F ast asleep, I dreamt I was in snowy Finland with the huskies around me
I n this land, where snow is deep landscapes are frozen and the wind blows strong
N ot in that land but in this land, snow and ice form under our feet
L and of snow, ice and wind, I wish I was there again, the land I love
A nd you can walk on ice because it's so cold in the frozen land
N ow on my count, we're off on a husky ride through the snow-capped trees
D o you know where I am? I'm in bed, in Finland, in the cold I love.

Beatrice Tailby (9)
Nun Monkton Primary Foundation School, York

A Place In My Dreams

There's a place in my dreams,
It's a magic land not far away from here,
The colours are bright like the moon and the sun,
And strange creatures are near,
I glanced around the twilight hills,
They surrounded me like a cloak, I saw a shadow and a noise,
A tiny little croak,
There stood before me a little thing,
Bright green with huge, round eyes,
Her long, floppy ears trailed on the ground
And she looked at me in surprise.

There was a funny feeling in my head.
I woke up safe and warm in bed.

Florence Shackleton (9)
Nun Monkton Primary Foundation School, York

Flying Through Your Dreams

Soaring into the midnight sky,
I found myself flying high.
Above white-tipped mountains and frozen lakes,
I glided over the landscape.
A magical feeling sprinkled through the air,
As the sky itself started to flare.
Into oranges and reds,
Pinks and purples,
The sun rose up into blurs and bubbles.
I woke up in my own warm bed,
As thoughts raced around in my head.
Could this be the start of a new adventure?
Could this be the start of a new future?

Winnie Jacob (10)
Nun Monkton Primary Foundation School, York

Dreaming Dreams

The dancing blue clouds,
That frolic through the pink sky,
That stretch so high.

Mountains bubbling,
The pops echo further than light,
They will never stop.

The water and sun,
Meet together and make one,
Beams of water light.

Dreams and emotions,
Thoughts and feelings are all there,
Dreams will never go.

Jasper Burdette (10)
Nun Monkton Primary Foundation School, York

Robin

R obin gracefully flutters like an elegant ballerina on ice
O ver the bleak moors, it flies through the dead of winter
B leak winter is the time when graceful robins come out so they can elegantly fly over the wet moist moors
I ntelligent, they always find their way home
N avigates the land like an air pilot in battle.

George Dunford (8)
Nun Monkton Primary Foundation School, York

Dream Dragons

D ragons, dragons everywhere
R ed skin, bright eyes and a ribbon-like tail
A ll I see in my sleep is dragons
G aze in wonder and see their wings
O h dragons, how you soar
N ever landing to see the intruders stalking their land
S o beautiful, so majestic, don't leave my world of dreams.

Elijah Ritchie (9)
Nun Monkton Primary Foundation School, York

The Opposite World Of Dreaming

Once upon a dream, I saw birds on the ground and cats in the sky.
Once upon a dream, I saw planes driving and cars flying.
Once upon a dream, I saw dogs walking and humans barking.
Once upon a dream, I saw fish walking and spiders swimming.
Once upon a dream, I saw cakes freezing and ice creams warming.

Ruby Buck (9)
Nun Monkton Primary Foundation School, York

Where Dragons Fly

Where dragons fly
Right before my eyes
I am all alone
But in the distance... a groan
Who could it be?
What could it be?
Where dragons fly
And witches cry
Happy little rainbow fills the sky
It doesn't make sense all this nonsense
What next...
Can pigs *fly?*

Seb Burdette (10)
Nun Monkton Primary Foundation School, York

Robin

R ed as a fire engine, round as a circle
O pen-beaked, sprinting, tiptoeing, fluttering
B eak pointed, sharp as a pencil
I n the sparkly snow, moving stealthily, fruit nibbler
N ow turns his head, moving stealthily with a high-sounding whistle.

John Turton (7)
Nun Monkton Primary Foundation School, York

Sweetie Land

Sweetie Land is real, I swear!
Well, I believe it's really there.
At night, I see it in my dreams,
And it's as perfect as it seems.

When you snuggle me up in bed,
Tuck away my sleepy head.
I drift away to Sweetie Lane,
The home of the scrumptious sugar cane.

You can even lick the bark of a tree;
It will taste like an orange sweetie.
In the centre of the land, there's a great big mountain,
But if you look closer, it's a chocolate fountain!

The clouds are made of cotton candy,
And for a snack, they're very handy.
The stones are made of Jelly Tots,
So if I fancy, I'll have lots!

All of my dreams have come true!
If only they could be shared with you.
If we lived in Sweetie Land,
Every day, we'd go hand in hand.

I have a friend there who's called Fred,
And he is made of gingerbread!
Now my dream is all over,
So I'll go back to my home in Dover.

Lottie Thorneycroft (9)
Orchard House School, Chiswick

Dragon Ride

Excitement tinged with curiosity dances within my body.
I am riding a breathtakingly magnificent red-scaled dragon.
His steely silver eyes shine in the velvety black night,
And his ruby-red wing tips brush the full moon as it smiles down at us.
I listen to the steady beat of his wings,
In perfect harmony with the twinkling of stars and whispering of pine trees below.
Cold air presses against my face.
When I look down I see a canvas of emerald green dusted lightly with snow.
I see blue frozen lakes in the forest that stretch on endlessly,
Into the horizon, where tall snow-capped mountains stand.
The warm comforting feel of the dragon and the rhythmic pulse of his wings,
Slowly let me close my eyes and go to sleep…
I wake, and there is no dragon or forest of pines.
There are no stars above my head.
It was only a dream but I remember it like it was real.

Iyla Stickney (9)
Orchard House School, Chiswick

Where Dreams Go

Whoosh! I was zooming,
Over moon, sun and far, far, away,
I splashed down in a dream nebulous.

A sea of glittering gases around me,
Of swirling colours, many.
Bobbing in the gases, white orbs were shining,
The size of large watermelons.

I plunged my head into one,
A lake of lava appeared.
An acrobatic crocodile was walking across it!

Into another, I peered.
A vampire in his underwear,
Singing fearlessly, "Don't go breaking my heart."

Then, suddenly, I fell into another orb and there was a change of scene,
In terror, I was being chased by a bulking ball.
The ball grew piercingly luminant,
Until it was a glowing, white orb.
"Darling, darling. It's time."

Lawrence Schmidt (10)
Orchard House School, Chiswick

Winning Wimbledon

I wouldn't mind winning Wimbledon,
Actually, it's my dream,
To hear the crowds cheer and whoop and scream,
To hear the commentator saying,
"He's done it, he's won the final match!
And the amazing skills he's displayed today,
Were more than up to scratch!"

My family and friends are all jumping for joy,
And it's all because of this one little boy,
Who once had a dream, and shot for the stars,
And got so far that he landed on Mars.

There's a message in this poem,
And that message is,
That no matter who you are,
You're allowed to have a dream,
And to make it come true,
As long as that dream,
Matters to you.

Michael Waller (10)
Orchard House School, Chiswick

Riding A Bike On Mars

I was doing it!
I, the first person to ride a bike on Mars, was succeeding,
I was amazed as the rock towers were as tall as towering turrets,
And the whole bike rattled as it went over some small rocks,
At one point I heard a creepy noise,
But it was just the wind whistling in my ear,
A while later the sand sang a lovely tune,
As it rustled around in the bright red and orange dunes,
My heart felt warm, unlike the weather,
When I stopped to look at a few stones which were miniature faces.

Amelia Arcos Lippens (9)
Orchard House School, Chiswick

Deep Down In The Ocean

Deep down in the ocean, there lives,
A treacherous urchin that is at will to kill at any cost.

Deep down in the ocean, there lives,
A diminutive fry who pitifully hides behind the fluorescent coral as the hungry creature advances in his voyage.

Deep down in the ocean, there lives,
An ornamental squid who frequently changes colour.

Deep down in the ocean, there no longer lives,
A skeleton fish who is currently in the stomach of a less-hungry squid.

Thomas Jenke (10)
Orchard House School, Chiswick

It Was All Just A Dream

As I lumber through the pitch darkness of the night,
Everything gives me a fright.
I can hear them incredibly near,
Now they can smell my fear.
Even though I am afraid,
I step out of the shade.
Luckily, I quickly dash,
But my sound makes a monstrous *crash*.
I can feel their vivid irritation,
There will hopefully be some relaxation.
After that, I see a majestic gleam,
But wake to find out it was all just a dream.

Theo Viall (9)
Orchard House School, Chiswick

Abandoned

All I can see is the back end of my ship,
They didn't give me any food, not a fruit, not even a pip,
Stuck on this sandy circle of land,
I could try swimming but they sawed off my hand,
Oh no! Watch out, shark attack!
It must think I'm a sizzling snack,
Suddenly I wake up and hear my sister driving me and my family around the bend,
Seven o'clock in the morning and the torture starts again.

Theo Cleanis (10)
Orchard House School, Chiswick

Demogorgans In The Night

Demogorgans in the night,
Always hiding in the blackness,
Have been terrified of the light,
Standing out because of abstractness.

Terrifying humanity as a hobby,
Lingering out in the alleyways,
Going into the lobby,
Still hungry, anyway.

Resting in the day,
So to pounce in the night,
Waking up at Nychthemeron,
As they prepare to bite.

Antonio Maisto (10)
Orchard House School, Chiswick

Dreamland

Unreal, this is
As I look around
Surrealist, these
Sights, smells and sounds.

The place to be
This special land
It has candy trees
And gem-like sands.

Everywhere, a
Friendly face
Personified, a
Unique space.

But you look scared
You've stand-up hair
'Cause round the corner
There's a nightmare!

Harry Rees (10)
Orchard House School, Chiswick

The Ballerina

She danced so gracefully across the room
Bathed in the entrancing light of the moon
I sucked in a breath when she passed by me
The ballerina's dance, so wild and free.

The dance came to her naturally
I wish I could dance so effortlessly
But sometimes our dreams do come true
I hope that you follow your dreams too.

Louisa Fay (10)
Orchard House School, Chiswick

Nightmare

Thud! Razor-sharp talons hit the ground,
A scarlet and teal dragon lands.
Fire erupts from his mouth,
Toxic fumes fill the air,
Charred, poisonous gases explode upwards.
People scream and cry,
Pandemonium hits the village.
Is it the end?
I wake up alert, shocked and startled.
It was all a nightmare.

Elsie Brimacombe (9)
Orchard House School, Chiswick

A Football Fan's Dream

When I walk to the stadium,
Fellow fans joke and cheer,
As I get to my seat,
I can feel my nervous heartbeat,
My heart soars,
When my team scores,
That winning feeling,
That nothing can beat,
And in my dream,
My team always wins the league.

Daniel Tovar (9)
Orchard House School, Chiswick

Dog Legend

Dogs were all, far and wide, sucked up a wormhole,
Into this dimension, the dimension of dreams,
And what was that? A house, fluff everywhere,
And lots of dogs to be friends with and have fun.

Over the sky, up and over and under,
Rainbow colours filled up the space around me,
I felt nervous about what was going to happen,
I saw something different all over and I rushed towards it.

My dog, Millie, she was sucked up a wormhole into this time,
She showed me gratitude and I fell to the ground in warmth,
We ran and ran 'til the day was nigh,
So we went to the house and fell asleep.

With all the stray dogs, who all now had a home.

Scarlett Robson Rose (10)
Queen Eleanor Primary School, Harby

The Lost

The Lost is a land where everything goes,
The Lost is a land where everything's thrown.
It's a place where things, big and small,
Get lost and are not found at all.
Once I fell in and was so freaked out,
I fell over and felt something crawling about.
One big spider weaving a web,
One big spider making a bed.
I jumped, I shuddered, I ran away,
I found an exit to make my day.
After I got out, I wandered around,
So I went back to town in a city that is loud.

Leila McCarthy (10)
Queen Eleanor Primary School, Harby

When I Grow Up I Will Be

When I grow up I will be losing fuel,
I'm so worried I'm kicking like a mule,
Let's land on Mars,
The red planet in the stars.

From our F16 we see the crazy cleaner,
Upon her shoulder rests a space lemur.
She shows us to our spacey room,
On her magical broom.

I say to Mum how cool,
But that cleaner is a fool,
We're at the Space Castle Inn, amazing,
And that cleaner is crazy!

Lawrence Bloor (10)
Queen Eleanor Primary School, Harby

The Exploration

I had just woken up in my room,
Though it felt like it was a tomb.
My house was a tall oak tree,
And now I was finally free.
At the top of the highest tree,
Exploring in the Amazon rainforest,
Although feeling like a tourist.
Trees and animals galore,
Wondrous to explore.
Wandering around in nature's imagination,
Everything looks like an animation.
All with my pet king cobra called Cobe.

Freddie Baker (9)
Queen Eleanor Primary School, Harby

Danger Zone

I'm in an F-16 and it's all about to go wrong
My copilot, Goose, says
"Are you ready to go?"
We are all lined at the runway and
Off we go
We are at our cruising altitude
And it goes wrong
We both eject
Then I survive but Goose dies.

George Barnard Hughes (10)
Queen Eleanor Primary School, Harby

Untitled

The light was green,
My engine roared with excitement.
I was catching up to second place,
And I won!
I was going to another race in America,
I drove off into the sunset.

Ewan Jenkins (9)
Queen Eleanor Primary School, Harby

In Space

In my dreams up in space, I see planets and stars and lots of universes.
Moving around, they float up and up, zooming faster and faster.
My rocket lands and the door pops open like a shooting star moving at the speed of light.
As I take my first step on the moon, the sun sings to me.
A spotlight from the sun lands on me.

In my dreams up in space, I meet an alien of lovely bright green.
I teach it to speak every language in every universe.
It talks now and we have a conversation about where we live.
"I live in a house made of water and it is bouncier than a trampoline."
"You can drink whenever you want."

In my dreams up in space, we summon gravity but then we change it back.
We collect rocks from the moon and then head back into the rocket.
On my way home, I see everything I need to see and everything is perfect.

In dreamland, you can be anything you want and do anything you want
Because in dreamland, anything is possible.

Willow Finnegan (9)
Shepherd Primary School, Rickmansworth

YouTuber

I'm in a mansion with twenty-five TVs so I'm never bored,
Zoom, my subscribers go up to ten million,
Outside, the ocean marries the sun as she keeps him warm,
The clouds are as soft as a marshmallow.

I'm in a mansion with twenty-five TVs so I'm never bored,
My mansion is made of green leaves and hard tree bark for a door,
I can see a bee, as yellow and black as day and night,
I'm rich and famous but that is not enough.

I'm in a mansion with twenty-five TVs so I'm never bored,
I'm a famous YouTuber but that won't help,
I'm not happy because I need more,
I need to help homeless people and people who are poor.

I'm in a mansion with twenty-five TVs so I'm never bored,
My money makes sure people are fed,
It makes sure people have shelter,
This is great!

Trishan Gupta (8)
Shepherd Primary School, Rickmansworth

The Day I Won

The day I won,
I felt amazing with the gold medal around my neck,
The crowd cheered, "Hurray! Hurray!"
I smiled happily along.

The day I won,
I felt amazing.
I remember when I zoomed across that floor,
I was more excited than ever and ready to win,
And I won first place.

The day I won,
I couldn't believe it.
Another gold medal to put on my shelf.
I thought I would lose like I always do,
But I won first place instead.

The day I won,
I felt like a star.
I dashed home to show my friends.
I was so happy when the crowd cheered for me,
I felt special and I won first place.

The day I won,
My first gold medal,

I won the whole competition too,
I felt amazing, like nothing could stop me.
I was so excited to be in first place.

Connie Moore (8)
Shepherd Primary School, Rickmansworth

I Won!

I won when everyone said I couldn't do it
I won when no one believed me.
I won when no one rooted for me.
I beat everyone!

I won and got everything I could ever need.
I won; I knew I could.
I won because I never gave up,
I kept my resilience; I kept my strength.

I wrote the best book in the world!

The crowd is cheering, I turn around.
They are so shocked, there's not a sound.
All those people who didn't believe.
The badge in my hand shows that I can achieve
Anything, when I believe.
I forgot about them and stayed happy.
But some people were quite snappy.
People shout at the top of their lungs.
While a beautiful song plays on the drums.

Scarlett Jones (9)
Shepherd Primary School, Rickmansworth

Footballer

On Mount Everest, there lies a gingerbread man who is me.
And I live in a flying fish with all the gods.
Then I end up winning the World Cup.
For the third time making the three stars ours.
Next, my snack comes and my snack is a cloud.
My snack is a cloud because it is cotton candy.

When we woke up on Mount Everest at 8 o'clock.
The sun happily smiled at us saying morning.
Then there was a party in another flying fish.
At the party, there were loads of balloons.
All I heard was pop and pop all the time.

When we left the fake waves waved goodbye.
Then the fires were hungry so I gave him some buttons,
Not my buttons because I'm a gingerbread man.
When I was home I heard fireworks.

Freddie Norwood (9)
Shepherd Primary School, Rickmansworth

Adventure Dreams

I went with my friend into the enchanted woods. We walked, we talked, we ran. It was an adventure.
N ot a sound in the woods to be heard with my friend, and we saw
V icious tigers approach, coming out of the bush.
E ach of us ran as fast as we could. Suddenly, we stopped.
N obody moved an inch. We saw light but we heard crying.
T hen I ran to see what was wrong. They had broken their game.
"**O** h no!" I said in shock. "What shall we do?" said my friend worriedly.
"**R** elax. I want to be an inventor so I can fix it." This is dreamland. Welcome!

Raeya Patel (8)
Shepherd Primary School, Rickmansworth

Art

A paintbrush in my hands,
R eady to draw for the King. He is very
T ense and is pleasant. He is looking forward to
I nspecting his portrait. The paint drips off the
S carlet-red paintbrush. My mum and dad are
T ending to me nervously. I have finished my
masterpiece.

D id the King like the picture? Yes, he did! He is
R adiant. He said I could stay for a meal.
E xcitedly, I say, "Thank you!" My mum
A nd dad are proud of me. They say, "Well done!
M agnificent." Yummy food is set on the table.

Leona Hetemi (8)
Shepherd Primary School, Rickmansworth

My Big Dream

F ootball is good, it's fun.
O liens are special aliens from Mars.
O liens are silly, they are fun!
T he planet Mars winks at the aliens.
"B attle the Oliens!" scream our players.
A liens are almost the same - green, tall.
L ionel Messi came to watch with Ronaldo.
L ionel Messi liked our tackles.
E arth was nothing like Mars - not always 500 degrees!
R eally, this was the best day ever!

Thomas R (9)
Shepherd Primary School, Rickmansworth

Dream Writer

Flying horses, flying fans.
Come along, I'll show you my plans.
Soon, I'll have my own poem,
As long as we hold hands.

My young voice is working away,
So I have to write it my way.
I hope this makes its way
To another small poet like me today.

I hope I made you happy,
I'm sorry if it was yappy.
I worked hard to achieve my dream,
You, too, can achieve your dream like me!

Michael Swalwell (8)
Shepherd Primary School, Rickmansworth

Being A Footballer

I woke up and I was on Saturn,
I saw a cheering stadium,
Then I saw Messi and Ronaldo,
They were scoring like a lion,
But then the cheering stadium talked to me.

I woke up and I was on Saturn,
Ronaldo was running like a cheetah,
Whoosh! Messi asked me to play on his team,
Ronaldo passed me the ball,
I ran, I scored,
We won the match.

Elis Byles (8)
Shepherd Primary School, Rickmansworth

In Paint Land

In Paint Land, you can draw anything you desire.
It comes out with a pop, and you have it in your hands.
In Paint Land, you draw clothes to wear,
A house to live in and, if you are lucky, draw a mansion!
In Paint Land, there is a paint teacher
Who teaches you how to paint.
In Paint Land, there is nothing to stop you,
Just believe in yourself, and have a go!

Sariyah Thomas (9)
Shepherd Primary School, Rickmansworth

Far From Free

In a forest with scarcely any light,
My body fills with dread and fright,
I look around, eyes filled with tears,
What I see confirms all my fears,
Now I know I'm far from alone,
There are others in this nightmare zone.

A crackling bonfire in front of my eyes,
Scattered around it are strange supplies,
I see a red pentagram under my feet,
Suddenly I'm filled with unpleasant heat,
Now before me, a person stands,
Holding a charm between their hands.

They start to chant and I hear a voice in my head,
"Hey! Get up! Get out of bed!"
I bolt upright in my room, panting with relief,
But my sense of security is brief,
Something lies on my bed in front of me,
I realise that I'm far from free.

Niamh Hackett (11)
St Macartan's Primary School, Clogher

Sleepovers

S cary stories, drinks and sweets, we are going to have an amazing night
L urking shadows, haunting screams, Scary Mary in candlelight
E erie sounds, creaking boards, getting splinters from the wooden floor
E veryone goes quiet, then there's a creak. I scream and say, "There's someone at the front door!"
P eople in tears, all huddled up praying this won't be the last thing we do
O n our own, no lovely parents who make us feel better when we have the flu
V ery loud footsteps coming up the stairs
E ach of our backs tingle with standing hairs
R ight then we know the person must be bad
S uddenly, the door opens and it's just my dad.

Aoibhe Meenan (11)
St Macartan's Primary School, Clogher

Great Dreams

G ood dreams we have each night,
R unning around in the daylight.
E very night we dream a new dream,
A nd sometimes they're not as good as they seem.
T ime to time we all have fun,

D inosaurs can be in your dreams, lying under the sun,
R ainbows can be in dreams too,
E veryone you ever knew.
A re all waiting on the moon for you,
M eanwhile, you're fighting with space monkeys, you argue.
S o when you finally arrived, everyone was fast asleep snoring.

Then I woke up and realised it was all a dream.

Aine McElroy (10)
St Macartan's Primary School, Clogher

The Bear And The Fairies

Over the hill, far away, a bear was ready to eat its prey
Famous fairies came to play but they didn't know who they would meet today
They were on the grass, they had a picnic
With cherries and berries and big blackberries
Then they heard a big loud roar.

And then, there, the bear they saw with crazy hair
He let out a roar and said, "I'm going to eat you."
The fairies did not know what to do
Then looking at the cherries, the fairies fed them to the bear
And the bear and the fairies became best friends.

Niamh Connolly (10)
St Macartan's Primary School, Clogher

Chasing

C hasing lions, coming out.
H ungry for chasing the people about.
A far in the den of the lion, there were also tigers and leopards.
S uperpowers were made by the leopards for the next night.
"I like it when we go out to chase," they all said. "Now it's time for you to go, tiger," said the lion.
"N othing can stop me," said the tiger.
G oing back to the den, the tiger saw the lion and leopards were very shocked. Who knows what will happen next?

Erin McKenna (10)
St Macartan's Primary School, Clogher

Lost In My Dream

I woke up in this weird-looking place,
I looked around but couldn't make out a face,
Wondering why everyone was looking at me,
Still confused, why could this be?

Wondering where I was, I asked for help,
No one responded, so scared I let out a yelp,
I was worried because I heard no news,
I started crying because I was scared and confused.

Shaking and shivering with fright,
But then this girl came up to me behind the light,
I realised it was just my mother,
I woke up from my dream and I was safe under my covers.

Ava McElroy (11)
St Macartan's Primary School, Clogher

One Zombie In The Jail

Once upon a time, I robbed the bank
Did I not mention I was a tank?
When the police came, he took me to jail
Everyone in the town tried to pay for my bail
After that, I could not cope
When I was tied to a rope
When the police said no bail
I had to stay in jail
Then the alarm started blaring
And the noise was kind of scaring
It was because of a zombie
There was a lot of pressure put on me
In the end, everyone was fried
Except for me, I actually died.

Senan McElroy (10)
St Macartan's Primary School, Clogher

Getting Lost In The Forest

In my dream, me and Priya were in the town,
Trying really hard to escape a clown.
Running and running, but we started to get a fright,
Now we'd found a torch, we had a little light.
Me and Priya were too fast for the clown,
And when we got away, there was a big frown.
It was the clown, letting out a big scream,
Then we woke up in our cosy beds, it was only a dream.

Alanagh Scott (11)
St Macartan's Primary School, Clogher

Football

F ans roaring in the stands.
O n the sidelines, coaches are making demands.
O ver the world goals.
T ogether everyone is not bored.
B alls are flying everywhere.
A ll referees are not very fair.
L ovely goals are scored by my team.
L ook at all the players with loads of steam.

Darcy Keenan (9)
St Macartan's Primary School, Clogher

The Footballer

F un to watch
O ver the moon with excitement
O rdering a pizza while it's half-time
T ogether as a team forever
B lasting with hope that they win
A ll the people cheering for their team
L oving the game
L iam the goal scorer had a very good aim.

Eoin McConnell (9)
St Macartan's Primary School, Clogher

The Possessed Clowns

C lowns chasing me all about
L oud bangs coming from their lookout
O verheard them making laughing callouts
W e turned off the power to make a blackout
N ow the clowns have made a strikeout
S uddenly, the clowns made a big, massive shootout.

Enda Moynagh (10)
St Macartan's Primary School, Clogher

Football

F un to watch and play,
O ver the moon in a day,
O ur team will always have a sub,
T ogether as a club.
B aller or not, you're still a player,
A lways angry after a loss,
L osing is not allowed,
L iverpool all the way.

Fionnán Welford (10)
St Macartan's Primary School, Clogher

The Rainforest

R ain drips down on the leaves of the trees
A nimals like snakes can be poisonous; be careful!
I nteresting flowers and other plants and trees
N ature and the plants are so shiny
F ragrant perfume from exotic flowers
O rchids are bright purple and they are enjoying the sun
R eflection off the water when you look at yourself
E xtraordinary animals can do amazing sounds
S pots of light glow like jewels
T rees with brittle bark full of bugs.

Harry Chester (6)
St Paulinus CE Primary School, Crayford

Rainforest

R ain dripping on the delicate flower.
A mazing alligators swimming in the river.
I nsects digging underground.
N ever allow deforestation of the Kapok tree.
F antastic orchids shining in the forest.
O verjoyed monkeys are celebrating.
R oaring lions leaping in the rainforest.
E xotic, emerald green frogs are hopping.
S hy sloths are hiding behind the trees.
T angled snakes are stuck on the trees.

Thaniesh Seyon (6)
St Paulinus CE Primary School, Crayford

Untitled

R are animals roar.
A bove the trees, there are colourful birds flying.
I nsects crawl on the ground.
N ew flowers grow tall.
F antastic tigers run quickly.
O ver the tree, little insects fly.
R eflections are shown when you are looking in the water.
E xtraordinary fishes have races in the water.
S trange plants sway all around.
T iny creatures go to bed in the dark night.

Lois Odelade (7)
St Paulinus CE Primary School, Crayford

Rainforest

R uby plants dangle in the air.
A mazing animals making their homes.
I nteresting noises echo everywhere.
N ever-ending as far as the eye can see.
F antastic secrets lurk under your feet.
O ver the jungle parrots glide so fast.
R are smells fill the air.
E xotic animals finding their prey.
S potted lights are dappled everywhere.
T iny creatures hide under the ground.

Ara Ibukunolu (7)
St Paulinus CE Primary School, Crayford

Inside The Rainforest

R ain that is very fresh.
A mazing flowers bloom very bright.
I nsects are crawling up the tree.
N ature is beautiful and new plants grow.
F ire red roses grow big and strong.
O vergrown flowers are very, very big!
R uby red reminds me of my favourite flower.
E xcited frogs jump up and down.
S nakes are slithering up the trees.
T arantulas are crawling everywhere.

Aubrey Gould (6)
St Paulinus CE Primary School, Crayford

Untitled

R ich leaves growing.
A nacondas slither down the big trees.
I nsects scuttle along the wet soil.
N atural flowers are attached to the bark.
F resh leaves are soaking wet.
O ld, brown trees are tall and set.
R ed flowers are so colourful.
E xotic flowers are light green.
S corching light is shining in my eyes.
T he haunted tarantula is creeping in the forest.

Justin Fearon (7)
St Paulinus CE Primary School, Crayford

The Rainforest

R ed poisonous flower.
A bove my head, there's a monkey on a tree.
I nsects are crawling on my feet.
N ever pick the plants because they're poisonous.
F rogs are jumping into the pond.
O ver the bushes, monkeys play.
R uby-red new plants grow.
E xcited snakes slithering over me.
S loths are staring slowly at me.
T arantulas are crawling everywhere.

Niyah Lewis-Battiste (6)
St Paulinus CE Primary School, Crayford

Untitled

R ain is falling from the sky.
A nimals roaring through the forest.
I nsects crawling all around.
N ew flowers sprouting from below.
F resh, bright leaves falling down.
O range orchids waving in the wind.
R eflection in the water sparkles in the night.
E merald, bright frogs with eyes.
S lithering snakes on the trees.
T ree frogs jump from tree to tree.

Reggie King (6)
St Paulinus CE Primary School, Crayford

Rainforest

R ich green leaves grow carefully.
A mazing animals run super fast.
I nsects are running all over the ground.
N ew flowers are growing carefully.
F orest leaves are falling very slowly.
O ld trees with brittle bark.
R ain falls like a shower.
E merald-green frogs jump very high.
S loths move very slowly.
T igers wait for night to come then they pounce.

Theodore Tite (6)
St Paulinus CE Primary School, Crayford

Untitled

R ising emerald and ruby flowers.
A mazing bright, wet leaves.
I ncredible howling monkeys.
N ature has bright tree frogs.
F antastic, colourful, bright, rare macaws.
O ver my head, I see colourful, bright birds.
R oaring, fast, scary tiger in the forest.
E merald, fresh, clear water.
S leepy, slow, lazy sloths.
T angled branches up into the sky.

Keziah Chege
St Paulinus CE Primary School, Crayford

Untitled

R ain is falling everywhere.
A nimals eat juicy leaves.
I nteresting flowers are on the ground,
N ew life is coming to the rainforest.
F rogs are leaping on the lilypads.
O ld trees have animals on the branches.
R uby-red flowers on the floor.
E xcellent trees carry birds on them.
S trong roots grow every day.
T iny animals live under leaves.

Jacob Harding (7)
St Paulinus CE Primary School, Crayford

Rainforest

R ain helps the plants to grow
A bove the bushes are lots of poisonous leaves
I love the colourful flowers
N ew flowers are grown in the mud
F rogs are jumping on the ground
O ver the plants lots of poisonous vines
R ed flowers smell beautifully
E xtraordinary sounds animals make
S tripy tigers are predators
T rees covered in brown bark.

Darcy Lincoln (6)
St Paulinus CE Primary School, Crayford

Untitled

R ed ruby flowers like jewels.
A bush canopy like a bright, small tree frog.
I love colourful parrots.
N ature is so cool.
F resh leaves grow all around.
O ver the lions, butterflies dance in the air.
R ich, rare flowers for the bees.
E xcellent, emerald flowers everywhere.
S loths swinging on the trees.
T he lions are roaring at me.

Lily-Grace Garner
St Paulinus CE Primary School, Crayford

Rainforest

R ain is refreshing.
A mazing animals everywhere.
I nteresting insects crawling around.
N ew flowers everywhere.
F antastic fruit grow on the tree.
O ver my head a monkey swings tree to tree.
R oaring jaguars everywhere.
E xotic emerald frog.
S nakes slither everywhere and wait for their prey.
T igers jumping tree to tree.

Roxie Fernandez
St Paulinus CE Primary School, Crayford

Animal Antics In The Amazon

R ich green leaves grow carefully.
A mazing, fast animals.
I nsects flying to the sky.
N ew, emerald, tangled, green leaves.
F lying butterflies flying.
O vergrown orchids grow
R ainforest with the forest floor.
E merald-green frog eating bugs.
S un streaming through the trees.
T owering, big, fat trees with green leaves.

Zachariah Bolawole (6)
St Paulinus CE Primary School, Crayford

The Rainforest

R ain pouring down. Rich leaves coming together.
A mazing animals above our heads.
I nteresting insects crawling on our feet.
N ature is beautiful!
F antastic, fresh flowers.
O rchids growing over our knees.
R uby-red flowers invading.
E xotic plants everywhere.
S trong leaves coming.
T iny bugs crawling.

Imran Hussain (6)
St Paulinus CE Primary School, Crayford

The Fun Amazing Forest

R ed parrots flying through the trees
A nimals hunting amazingly
I nsects crawling on the floor
N ew birds sleeping
F lowers flowing
O ver the trees, the sun is shining
R oaring tigers are hunting
E very flower smells nice
S nakes slithering around on the ground
T igers growling to each other.

Noelle Omotoso (7)
St Paulinus CE Primary School, Crayford

Untitled

R are drops on the trees.
A bove the trees the birds fly.
I nsects go up on the tall trees.
N ever go near a leopard.
F orest is like a jungle.
O ver the bush, frogs jump.
R ainforest is wild.
E very animal might be dangerous.
S trong trunks have twigs.
T rees are strong and tall.

Ronnie King (6)
St Paulinus CE Primary School, Crayford

Untitled

R ich gold leaves
A mong the trees monkeys swing
I nsects crawl on the ground
N ature has lots of trees
F resh fantastic plants
O ver the fence, there is a frog
R oaring leopards running
E xtraordinary plants and bushes
S trong branches hold sloths
T iny ants crawl on the trees.

Jonatans Smirnovs (6)
St Paulinus CE Primary School, Crayford

The Dream

R ain is falling from the sky.
A delicate flower grows.
I nsects are crawling around.
N oisy, huge animals stomp.
F orest is so beautiful.
O ld trees with brittle bark.
R uby flowers all around.
E xtraordinary animals.
S quawking birds everywhere.
T he towering tree giants.

Rumer Cotton (7)
St Paulinus CE Primary School, Crayford

Magical Forest

R ich and shiny leaves.
A bove the tall trees.
I nsects are flying.
N ever cut the trees.
F riendly animals watching.
O rchids are so beautiful.
R ubies are shiny and red.
E xcellent animals.
S trange trees are growing.
T ired animals are sleeping.

Ethan Matthews (6)
St Paulinus CE Primary School, Crayford

Rainforest

R ed poisonous leaves
A mazing flowers grow
I nsects crawl in the mud
N ew sprouts push out of the soil
F resh leaves are wet
O val leaves unfold
R uby flowers grow tall
E yes gleam in a bush
S nakes slither on the ground
T igers hide in bushes.

Max Smith (7)
St Paulinus CE Primary School, Crayford

Everything Is Different

R ain is dropping down.
A nimals are sleeping.
I nsects crawling everywhere.
N ice trees grow pretty.
F rogs are poisonous.
O ver the tree birds fly.
R ed parrots fly up.
E meralds are shiny.
S lithering snake.
T he trees are growing in nature.

Billy Clarke (6)
St Paulinus CE Primary School, Crayford

Rainforest

R ain helps the plants
A nimals walk around
I nsects hide up the tree
N ature is beautiful
F resh leaves grow
O rchids, red and yellow
R uby flowers grow
E xotic plants grow everywhere
S nakes slither around
T iny bugs everywhere.

Lily-Ann Wombell (7)
St Paulinus CE Primary School, Crayford

My Imaginary Island

On a magical island, far and near,
Wonders await, have no fear.
Golden sands beneath our feet,
A place where dreams and adventures meet.

Waves that giggle, splash and play
Greeting the shore in a rhythmic ballet.
Palm trees whisper, secrets sweet,
As the sun and moon take turns to greet.

Butterflies dance in the warm sunlight,
Painting rainbows, a colourful sight.
Fairies twirl, leaving trails of spark,
This magic island's magic casts its enchanting reign.

Caves and coves hide treasures rare,
Guarded by shells, beyond compare.
Adventure whispers in the coconut trees,
A playground of joy carries the breeze.

Farhan Hussain (11)
Steeton Primary School, Steeton

Wrestling

I dream of being in the ring
Ready to fight at the sound of the bell's *ting, ting.*
My favourite wrestler is John Cena
I wonder if he's related to a Tina.
I'm too scared to talk about the Undertaker
He's the 'Deadman', what a faker
This one's a legend, known as Hulk Hogan
But I can't think of his slogan.
Let's talk about Ric Flair
At his age, he has amazing hair.
I wonder if you remember the Legion of Doom
So long ago, makes my brain go *boom!*
The tribal chief, aka Roman Reigns
He's very strong, probably could lift cranes.

Mohammed Ehsan Jameel (11)
Steeton Primary School, Steeton

Monsters Galore

Monsters galore
I happen to see more
From guinea pig goats
And dinos in moats
Or dragons which scare
And a tall, pink bear
But the scariest of all
You don't want to brawl
They happen to crawl
Not very tall
Then it comes towards me
A tiny spider as happy as can be
I wake up to see it was all a daydream
Then Mum called me to eat some cake and cream.

Mya Rodgers (10)
Steeton Primary School, Steeton

My Cat

My cat is called Mitten,
And she is a kitten,
She lives in Britain.
She bites a lot,
And I put her in a cot,
She plays with a sock
And I clean her up with a mop.
She hides in a pot a lot.
Her favourite toy is a mouse,
Called Pandty, she is always energetic,
I love Mitten and she is a kitten.

Emilia Quattrocchi (7)
Steeton Primary School, Steeton

Gramps And Cat

The stars were bright
In the dead of night
Not a sound was heard
Everyone was sleeping
Even the tiniest of birds.

Raindrops poured
As the old man snored
Waking up the cat next door
With a crash and a bang
The little cat ran
And the old man snored no more!

Daisy Marley (11)
Steeton Primary School, Steeton

YOUNG WRITERS INFORMATION

We hope you have enjoyed reading this book – and that you will continue to in the coming years.

If you're a young writer who enjoys reading and creative writing, or the parent of an enthusiastic poet or story writer, do visit our website **www.youngwriters.co.uk**. Here you will find free competitions, workshops and games, as well as recommended reads, a poetry glossary and our blog.

If you would like to order further copies of this book, or any of our other titles, then please give us a call or visit **www.youngwriters.co.uk**.

Young Writers
Remus House
Coltsfoot Drive
Peterborough
PE2 9BF
(01733) 890066
info@youngwriters.co.uk

YoungWritersUK   YoungWritersCW
youngwriterscw   youngwriterscw